Diva

Rafael Campo

DIVA

Duke University Press

Durham & London

1999

For my patients
who never waited for death

For Jorge
who always gives me breath

Contents

Acknowledgments   ix

I In the Cuban Way

The New World's History in Three Voices   3
The Repeating Island   4
Sonnet in the Cuban Way   6
The Return   7
The Dream of Loving Cuba   8
The Cardiac Exam   10
Suicidal Ideation   11

II Baby Pictures

Madonna and Child   15
Night Inexpressible   16
The Pelvic Exam   17
Baby Pictures   19
Diva   32
A Poet's Education   34

III The Gift of AIDS

The Gift of AIDS   39
The Abdominal Exam   40
Darkest Purple   41
The Changing Face of AIDS   42
A Death Perplexing   60
Small Comfort   61
Drawing Blood   62

IV *The X Files*

Opposites Attract   65
My Reasoning   66
Three Recent Films   67
Marry Me   72
Recognition   73
The Mental Status Exam   75
The X Files   76
Still Monogamous after Fourteen Years   77
Begging for Change in Winter   78
Last Rites   79

V *Lorca*

I Am Mrs. Lorca   83
Sonnets of Dark Love *(Translated from the Spanish of Federico García Lorca)*   84

A Note on the Translations   97

Acknowledgments

I am grateful to the editors of the following periodicals, in which some of the poems contained in this volume have appeared, sometimes in slightly different forms: *AGNI, Bostonia, The Boston Book Review, Boulevard, DoubleTake, The Five Fingers Review, The High Plains Literary Review, Hopscotch, The Lancet, Luna, The Marlboro Review, The Massachusetts Review, Ploughshares, Poz, Prairie Schooner, The Progressive, Salamander, Slate*, and *The Threepenny Review*.

"Sonnet in the Cuban Way" appeared in *El Coro: A Chorus of Latino and Latina Poetry*, edited by Martín Espada (University of Massachusetts Press, 1998). "Recognition" appeared in *Blood and Tears*, edited by Scott Gibson (Painted Leaf Press, 1999). "Darkest Purple" appeared in *The Beacon Best of 1999: Writing by Women and Men of All Colors* (Beacon Press, 1999).

I am also grateful to the John Simon Guggenheim Memorial Foundation for its generous support of this work.

In the Cuban Way 1

The New World's History in Three Voices

Confusing Cuba with a wealthy land,
Columbus started what for centuries
has plagued the people who survived in me:
part-slave, part-royalty, part-Caliban,

cross-dresser in the golden silk the sea
rolls out along a beach that isn't mine,
American yet un-American
because not one of us is truly free,

I am compelled to sing in rhyme
forgetting what the end of beauty is.
I know that beauty is both grand and wise;
I know that Cuba's dying is a crime

that started with Columbus and his lies.
The Caliban in me will dance as if
he understands that beauty is like love;
the royalty in me could do with less,

but always wants whatever he can have.
Today, I think I'm just as beautiful
as something I convince myself I feel
but can't remember, what the proud black slave

in me would call "the greatest gift of all."
I don't know what she means by that, her hands
so calloused none are more American,
but sing for this island, this miracle.

The Repeating Island

The culture of the Peoples of the Sea is a flux interrupted
by rhythms which attempt to silence the noises with which their
own social formation interrupts the discourse of Nature.
Antonio Benítez-Rojo

In Cuba, 1949, a boy
Who almost was a man, who lived beneath
A mountain where guerillas hid, so green
And full of shrieking parrots—children hid,
The sea murmuring, murmuring like the dead

So close beneath the mountain that was green,
All colors gathered in the jungle's arms.
The children playing, hiding, shrieks and laughs,
He played with them among the trees and snakes.
The trees that hid the renegades by night,
The snakes their wives made into soup,
The angry men who came by night to steal,
The men who smelled of liquor, black as night,
The traitors, rapists, pigs who stole their eggs
And chickens, killed the cows his father raised.
One day, they'd come to steal the whole nation,
The waves repeating, repeating what they said.

A boy one day, his country's fate the next,
In Cuba, vast plantations all around,
The sugar and molasses, white and brown,
The sugar cane like bullwhips in the wind,
The coffee quiet on the mountainsides—
Plantations framed by mountains and the sea,
Plantations where a kind of slavery
Made sweetness from the blackest sin,
Made bitterness from the sweat of men,
Refinement white as sugar, white as sand,

Dissolving in the coffee brewed so black.
The children playing, playing in the sun:

The men who stole, his people said, were men
More black than brown, whose children played and starved
And waved the Cuban flag. One story goes
There was a little boy, a boy who was
As lonely as a solitary star,
The boy who beat a young mulatto girl,
The beating, beating like the ocean's heart,

Accused of stealing while the children played,
A parrot shrieking, then the rifle shot—
He tried to save what was already lost.
My father tells me that they lost so much.
(I love my father, like I'm lost, so much.)
My father was his father's son, they owned
A vast plantation. Cuba: mountains, sea,
The vast plantation where a boy became
A man—in 1949, soon, soon,
A new divided nation would be born,
A new divided nation would be born.

Sonnet in the Cuban Way

To make you fall in love with me, I'd curse
Before I'd sing to you; implacable
And elegant, I'd force you with my class
Beneath a music kind of tropical
But mine enough you'd never recognize
Its foreign cadences. O island whore,
I'd stare like moonlight in your eyes,
I'd lie that I don't want you anymore
Then fuck you like Americans know how—
To make you fall in love with me, I'd die
Just near enough to you there'd be no doubt
My feelings are eternal. Dressed in dew,
You'd meekly pardon my brutality,
In love at last, so naked you'd seem free.

The Return

He doesn't know it yet, but when my father
and I return there, it will be forever.
His antihypertensives thrown away,
his briefcase in the attic left to waste,
the football game turned off—he's snoring now,
he doesn't even dream it, but I know
I'll carry him the way he carried me
when I was small: In 2023,
my father's shrunken, eighty-five years old,
weighs ninety pounds, a little dazed but thrilled
that Castro's long been dead, his son impeached!
He doesn't know it, dozing on the couch
across the family room from me, but this
is what I've dreamed of giving him, just this.
And as I carry him upon my shoulders,
triumphant strides across a beach so golden
I want to cry, that's when he sees for sure,
he sees he's needed me for all these years.
He doesn't understand it yet, but when
I give him Cuba, he will love me then.

The Dream of Loving Cuba

The island wants me back. It's half-erect
beneath America on all my maps—
just look at how it wants me, shamelessly,
a geographic urge that can't be helped,

a crime of nature, both a heretic
and ever faithful to its needs. I hate
to see it bargaining for amnesty,
as if this long seduction were the trip

I'll never take to see its shores, as if
to watch the ocean while it masturbates
with every stroke of curling wave could seem
like human hope. I know that it's a trap—

I know the island wants me to be rough,
to tell it that I'm never coming back,
to hate the jungles it puts on for me,
to throw the ripened plantains it prepares

across a room my father ate in once,
a room in a decrepit house in Cuba's locked,
unwilling past in which I dream. I dream
I'm bargaining for something we revere,

like freedom or redemption, and by chance
I come across a map I think I recognize—
unfolding it, I squelch the urge to scream,
until I see it tells me where desire

is. Cuba, take me back! I know that look,
I know you want me, begging on my knees,
to tell the truth of one lost history,
a truth I tell myself, your grateful liar.

The Cardiac Exam

Before the brainless heart gives out,
I realized while listening
To hers—I guess I understood
Its plaintive language passably,

Unlike the Spanish from her mouth,
That drowning, soft, unloosened song—
It wants to do some lasting good,
It wants never again to bleed,

It wants to float up just outside
The lonesome body that contains it.
To swell with joyful empathy,
Re-tell the cancer's seeding of

Her pericardium—a wide
Expanse of sweetest Cuban fruit
That feeds starved throngs, not emptiness
Unfilled by muffled beats of love

So distant I begin to hear
The music of a dying few,
Of how not one of us survived
Their murders, bodies choking swamps.

The germ of knowledge is in here:
Her failing organ is in you
Just as in me, her blue-green eyes
One world, a promise to be kept.

Suicidal Ideation

for Rafael Fernando Campo, d. 1993

Miami, near a hundred-eight degrees.
If temperatures were distances, by now
We'd see it, Cuba's razor edge, we'd see

The first few seagulls. Lowered in the ground,
What else is there to understand of him:
For years I thought he was the Cuban town

I never would inhabit, that his names
Were metonyms I never would decode.
The scorching sunlight, from behind them, limns

The wreaths of flowers in the finest gold;
The buzzing voices of the mourners, black
And secretive as flies. More lies are told.

My deep anxiety, I know, is back.
If suicidal ideation is
A nation that's both tropical and bleak

I know I've been there: long before the wars
Of shame, I razed the island that he was.

Baby Pictures **11**

Madonna and Child

By menopause, it's not just estrogen
my mother lacks. She's lost her eldest son—
that's me, the one who's queer—the doctor who
once made her very proud. These days, I do
my own wash when I'm home, I cook for her
so she can take a break from all the chores
she now refuses to assign to me.
She sits, half-watching Ricki through her tea's
thin steam, her squint of disapproval more
denial than it is disgust. She hears
much better than she sees—it's easier
to keep out vision than it is to clear
the air of sounds—and yet I know it's age
that stultifies her senses too. Enraged
because she's lost so much, I understand
why suddenly she looks so stunned
as from the television: ". . . Bitch, she stole
my boyfriend, my own mother did! . . ." I fold
a towel noiselessly. I know she thinks
it's garbage, sinful, crap—just as she thinks
that taking estrogen in pills is not
what God intended, no matter what
the doctors say; or that I'm gay is plain
unnatural, she can't endure such pain.
The oven timer rings. The cookies that
I've baked are done. I'll make another batch
though she won't touch them: given up for Lent.
My mother's love. I wonder where it went.

Night Inexpressible

in memory of Audre Lorde, d. 1994

Before it was malignancy, before
You wrote the poetry I know you as,
You had a woman's body. Warmed by fires

I tremble to awaken, through the smash
Of rioters outside your door you lived
Without mirrors, swallowed broken glass

Until your instrument was sharp enough,
Then bravely ventured out to sing the blues.
You told it all: the women whom you loved,

The facts of an oppression still as cruel
As slavery, the cancer in your breast.
Your woman's body, black as it was true,

Withstood much more than we could bear. Your breath,
As I walked home last night: the library,
Dark wind through trees? I strain against your death,

Much greater than a single casualty—
In a gust, a vast, black woman embraces me.

The Pelvic Exam

The speculum is silvery and cold.
The uterus has secrets to be told.
Abnormal bleeding after periods:

Blighted pregnancy, or cancer taking hold,
Infection, trauma silently withstood.
My speculum is silvery and cold,

Its jaws are open to the source of blood.
It enters her. Vaginal walls unfold.
"Abnormal bleeding after periods—"

I stop myself. "You're seventeen years old?"
She shivers as my fingers poke and prod.
My speculum is silvery and cold;

I look away from it to see her nod.
At first, the tears that drop are half-controlled.
Abnormal bleeding after periods

Has made her pain's unwilling centerfold,
The child I would safeguard if I could.
The speculum is silvery and cold,

The brute examination it allowed
Not consolation, more a wordless scold.
Abnormal bleeding after periods

Can only be so many things. Withheld
Until she knows, her sobs become a flood.
The speculum is silvery and cold

Upon the table where it sits, the blood
Now dried. This case, before you ask, is closed:
Abnormal bleeding after periods.
The speculum is silvery and cold.

Baby Pictures

I. Imaginary

Now that we are mostly in our early thirties, it seems that so many of my friends from medical school are rushing to get pregnant and have babies—while all I have given birth to in these past three years is utterly imaginary. I suppose reproduction must seem all the more imperative from where we stand, uncertain, at the brink of the next millennium. We have the appropriately awesome technology, though: my friend Jonna, unable to conceive after two years of trying, recently underwent IVF and is now carrying twins. Last week I was thinking about those two miraculous embryos swimming inside her pink uterus, and it struck me that the two books of poems I have published bear a rather haunting resemblance to one another. I felt defensive for a moment, if not exactly parental, comparing my oranges to her apples. Though at times I felt my poems quicken inside me, their physiologic iambs an emanation of my own life-force, their small stanzas as recognizable and uniquely shaped as new-born's hands, I knew immediately that what I had created was alive in a different way. Though I had felt the pangs of their creation in my mouth and in my heart, their "birth" each time resulted in a thing that did not cry or pee or feed. They were words, without urges or needs. Each poem, I suddenly realized, was birth itself, or a backwards kind of birth, inertly requiring the same painful process be repeated every time it entered the consciousness of another reader, which was what made it so monstrous, so unreal, so unimaginable.

II. AIDS Mother

When she refused my suggestion that she have an abortion, I was annoyed. Odds were she would transmit the virus to her unborn child, since she also wouldn't take AZT. She explained that because her fiancé had left her when he found out she was HIV infected, and because she would probably die soon, that giving birth to this child would be the only record of the existence of their love. That baby in her womb would transform the dark ghetto inside her into a beautiful forest, and it would come out all clean and sparkling new, not toxic! Even if the baby was born with AIDS, she would take care of it as best she could. She would be a good and loving AIDS mother, not like some who just deserted their innocent little ones in the delivery ward, in a hurry to get back on the streets and use. She would make sure that if the baby outlived her, that her parents back in Cuba would take it in after she died—that she would keep writing to them and prove that she wasn't a whore and a dirty shooter any more. Her healthy baby would make them love her again, and she pictured her own mother at her side squeezing her hand during the contractions, tears streaming down her face, remembering her same agony as she gave birth to the woman with HIV in bed beside her, the sweet, sweet daughter she had never really abandoned.

III. *Aliens*

In the check-out line at the Lil' Peach, I saw the headline: WOMAN
RECALLS HER OWN BIRTH—BY ALIENS! The most inaccessible of memo-
ries laid bare, reported as publicly as Oprah's denial that she is homo-
sexual and how to lose thirty pounds in three days and keep it off. The
Mexican man with a ponytail in front of me was buying a carton of New-
port menthol cigarettes. I tried to imagine his birth, his first cry powered
by pristine lungs, sound from across the most fundamental of borders. An
elderly white woman with a wig arranged crookedly on her head walked
past the store's door. I tried to imagine her birth, her illiterate mother's
surprise at the otherworldly bald head of her newborn. As I approached
the counter to be rung up, I remembered the black woman I'd tried to
ignore sitting on the sidewalk at a street corner as I went about my er-
rands. She was selling a pair of shoes that looked like they were fished
from someone's trash; I tried to imagine her learning to walk, though
when I actually saw her I'd wished she'd never been born at all. As I paid,
unforgiving and shameless voyeur, I thought I understood if just for a mo-
ment what we all have in common—and why we all remain so intently
strangers to one another.

IV. Prom Queen

A few nights ago I had a terrible nightmare. I dreamed I was that prom queen from New Jersey who gave birth to her baby in a lavatory. I watched myself as I smoothed down my dress, exited the chrome stall, and discarded the limp thing in a plastic trash barrel. I covered it with some handfuls of scrunched-up brown paper towels. A toilet flushed in another stall as I looked at myself in the wall-length mirror, fixing my hair and dabbing on some make-up. I was thinking. I was surprised it wasn't bloodier, but my dress was so red that it might have obscured some of the mess. I was surprised it wasn't more painful, but since I had never had a vagina before, I supposed I might not know how to interpret any pain I was feeling. Then I remembered my boyfriend, how much I enjoyed sucking his cock. I did feel a little slick between my legs. I wondered whether swallowing too much come could get a girl pregnant, since I'd only let him push it inside me once or twice. Somehow at that point I realized I was a doctor, and though it didn't make sense since I was only in high school, I decided I didn't have to worry about it anymore. It was all over. I strolled out of the bathroom, a little nervous but very natural, and noticed two policemen were making out on the dance floor, which made me suspect immediately that someone was on to me, that I was wrong. The gymnasium was as big and empty as my heart felt, and the streamers and balloons seemed childish and stupid. So I started dancing alone to a song I've always hated by that high-strung, uppity bitch Celine Dion, and that's when I began to cry uncontrollably. I realized that all the awful noise was the same primitive, hopeless wail my baby had made before I had killed it. I woke up with a start, in a cold sweat.

V. Barren

When I was a young child, I remember my mother explaining to me why one of my aunts had never given me any cousins to play with, though she and my uncle had wanted a baby very much. I was worried about what evil might befall anyone who did not procreate; in my mother's large Italian family, everyone seemed to marry before they finished school and immediately started their own families. My mother said very quietly that my aunt was barren, which meant she could never, ever have children. I was stunned by the hard fact that God would make anyone incapable of the miracle of childbearing. Of course, as a Catholic I immediately assumed she was being punished for some ungodly sin (probably the sin of having sex without the purpose of making babies), and I believed how she accepted her fate would be the test of her worthiness to be saved in the end. Yet I was also consoled by this knowledge. I imagined my poor aunt had the same poisoned womb God had given me: I too wanted to be a mother, even though I had been cruelly teased for being "queer" by my brothers when I played with baby dolls. For many years after this revelation, I secretly imagined I was the child my aunt could never bear, at once alive and the denial of life, the joy she would never feel and deprived of the same potential for joy, as bereft as she was, fulfilling the thwarted promise of my mysterious inheritance.

VI. Demeter

The first birth I attended during my medical training occurred at around 3 A.M., on a night I was on call with a resident I didn't very much like. His first question to me was almost a threat: "So, how many have you caught?" When I answered "None," he sneered a little and started ranting that when medical students were on with him he didn't let them cower in the corner of the delivery room, and so I had better prepare for some action. He gestured to a labor room with a long Greek name posted in block print outside its door. "I want you right there between her legs when she goes. It should be an easy one, she's a G10 P7 Tab 2. Multips are a piece of cake." After some simple arithmetic, I figured out that he meant this delivery would be her eighth. Yawning, I headed toward the vending machine that dispensed Snickers bars and potato chips to get a snack to bring to the doctor's lounge where I planned to do a quick review of my pocket obstetrics manual. But before I could insert the first quarter, my mountainous patient (whom I'd never met) was being wheeled into the nearest delivery room, and my obnoxious resident was shouting, "Get your ass in here *now!*" As I hurried over, I thought briefly of one of my heroes, William Carlos Williams, and imagined through a composite of his poems and narratives the scene that awaited me: an ill-educated, screaming woman, a compassionate but reserved doctor saving her and her imperiled child, the difficult birth a metaphor for the discovery of meaning in life through poetry. What greeted me instead was the blaze of spaceship-like OR lights, the lesbian midwife I'd met earlier who glared at me contemptuously, and what I guessed was my resident beneath layers of disposable gowns, goggles, and a gauzy blue hairnet. The patient did not scream, and in fact spoke English perfectly, introducing herself with a cheerful laugh while I stared, paralyzed and dumbfounded, into her splayed-open crotch. I thought her vagina was huge, and her thick black pubic hair gave it a weird resemblance to the long face of her jovial, bearded husband who followed all of us into the room. My resident slapped a pair of latex gloves into my hands, and shoved me to the foot of the bed. A large metal bowl clanged like a church bell as it hit the floor between us, and the infant was so slippery I nearly dropped her into it when she was forced out by a single barely visible effort by her mother, whose muffled grunt was accompanied by a quiet fart. I mistook the umbilical cord for a tail, horrified for a few moments until the midwife clamped it and I realized what it was. Most surprising was the warm gush of blood that immediately preceded the delivery of the placenta. "I know she's fine, stupid," I heard the mother say to her husband as the pediatrician documented the Apgar scores. "Now get over there and have them bring me my beautiful little girl, my perfect Demeter."

VII. August

My sister was born when I was almost fourteen years old, and my mother was almost forty. When the amniocentesis was done, my brothers and I shuddered to think of someone inserting that long needle pictured in the pamphlets my parents had brought home from the doctor's office into the great white egg of my mother's pregnant belly. I remember the nervous conversations while the final test results were processed; the ultrasound had been reassuring, and through the swirls and static the images had revealed my mother was carrying a girl, her first daughter. *She will be in the Class of 2000 when she goes to college. She will look like Aunt Mary. She will be left-handed like you almost were.* We dared not imagine any defects, that her heart might be slightly imperfect, or that her spinal cord might not have sealed shut properly, or that the infinitesimal weight of an extra chromosome carried from the moment of conception might keep her from going to college at all. August came, and my mother promised God she would never drink coffee again if the baby turned out fine. When my sister arrived at home from the hospital swaddled in her embroidered pink blanket, and I watched my mother feed her the milk from her own body, as tenderly as if her breast were weeping and the child's mouth was its only solace, I knew all the worrying had been for naught. My sister existed, her birth linking that long summer to a distant point in the future: someday soon, I would recognize her face; in a time equal to the life I had lived until then, she would be a young woman preparing for college, the Class of 2000, a place so far away I could almost imagine peace.

VIII. Fucking

I think I know what birth feels like. Not literally, of course. It's the pleasure of such an intimate commerce with the outside world, of imagining oneself extending eternally into the world, of not so much immortality but fundamental renewal of the self, that I feel, or remember. I would never want actually to have a baby. But I love to be a mother when I'm fucking, or being fucked, I love to think in those moments of crossing into another state of consciousness, in the palpitations and the dizziness and the rhythmic pressure around my cock that makes me cry out and the tingling around my mouth, in the words he's murmuring in my ear that don't make any sense at all except to my innermost mute organs, in the hallucinations that I'm hurtling through interplanetary space that may or may not have to do with having listened to Karen Carpenter who I realized spookily is dead now earlier in the evening, that none of this really matters besides what we produce together, not a child but the child's irreducible ecstasy, what each one of us felt at the first moment after birth.

IX. Doctor Kevorkian

At the hospice, there was a bowl of jelly beans on the coffee table in the TV room. A patient of mine was sitting there with me, dying of breast cancer while she watched a rerun of *Bonanza*, a show that stopped airing new episodes before I was born. One of the show's handsome young stars died of pancreatic cancer when I was still in medical school. I remember that she asked me during a commercial if I would give her a prescription for some pills. She was scared of dying alone, in pain. I told her that I was no Doctor Kevorkian, but that I believed it was my job to help her die with dignity. She said that death should be like birth, with family and friends all around you, medicine to keep you comfortable until it was all over, and a doctor at your side in case of any complications. I couldn't look at her; the more I stared at the jelly beans, the more they began to look like a bowl of multi-colored pills, benzodiazepines and narcotics and antidepressants, all the sweet flavors of relief. She began to cough by the time the show came back on, a deep rattle that made the soft sound of my own breathing unnerving to me. I had to attend a certain number of births during my medical training, but not deaths; the hospital where I worked published annual statistics on the number of babies born on its maternity ward, but the number of deaths each year was guarded like an embarrassing secret. I looked at my cachectic patient reflected in the television's gruesome single eye: its convexity shrunk and deformed her to the size of a plump fetus, and she was grinning at a robust Michael Landon, her image superimposed upon his large white teeth which looked like they were the whitest teeth the world had ever known, and I understood that in death she was traveling back to her own pure beginning. That in death she would be reborn.

X. Baby Pictures

A friend of mine, a poet, is leaving his wife and three-year-old daughter. I have a baby picture of his daughter stuck to my fridge with a fruit magnet. I used to watch him with her, feeding her some wedges of a green apple, or teaching her the meaning of a new word, and feel vaguely jealous. In them I saw the loss of my own newness, the distance I had achieved from my own birth. I couldn't feel their wonder. (In an album I never open, I have baby pictures my mother sent me of myself, black-and-white relics whose creases and yellow edges alarm me.) She was his way of being born over and over again into the changing world; each new taste, each discovery as much his as it was hers. Her birth was so powerful it might even have remade his marriage. When I gazed at her tiny face in the morning before taking out the milk for my cereal, that's what I secretly hoped, in spite of myself.

XI. Hysterectomy

When my uterus was removed, no surgery was required. When my child was born, they took her away from me, but at least my lack of a womb obviated a Caesarian section—that was one difficult birth! My name is Hysterectomy Gynelotrimin, and I myself was born in Ohio. I don't remember any of it, really, except for that man with the mask and the rubber gloves. When he put his hands inside me, they felt like cold steel and he reached so far up in there he could have been probing the planet Mars with his laser beams or something. Whole universes exist within our hearts, you know. I see them when I try to picture my daughter. They tell me I'm crazy, that once I made the neighbor boy climb inside my parents' refrigerator and I locked him in. That's bullshit. Every day when I wake up, I stare into the dawn and the cottony clouds that try to soak it all up and I try to understand what they did to me. I try to understand why they took her away. It's not like it was the end of the world coming out between my legs, it wasn't obscene like that. Hey, I'm an American citizen, this is the cradle of civilization in case anyone forgot, and I've got my rights. I've just got to find my baby, she wants to climb back inside me where it's safe, before some stranger gives birth to her, before this whole fucking country goes to the dogs. I love her, don't you get it? They can't sterilize me: giving birth to her was like the most incredible and permanent music in the world, going on inside your own body. I know she's out there somewhere, looking for me, singing our song at the top of her lungs.

XII. *Epiphany*

I want to go back to that small pond. I want just to stumble upon it again, behind a disintegrating barn in western New Jersey, where my cousins and I often played, stabbing sticks upright into the muck of its shore, bird calls falling softly on us like the first drops of a rain storm threatened by the darkening sky overhead. I want to study the shape of the footprint I left behind there, and then wish it away, so that it might yet be made. I want to go back now, and not harm a thing, not know a single species. I was there before the frogs began to vanish, at what seemed like the very edge of the known world. Once I found a great foamy mass of eggs embedded in clear jelly, attached to some scraggly reeds, the embryonic tadpole inside each one in some kind of suspended animation. Tense, alive but not, awaiting birth. It was so still I thought I had discovered the origin of all life. I thought of what the world expected of us— what the living make. The eggs shuddered slightly with a passing breeze. As much as I've wanted to, I never went back to that small pond.

Díva

Before I knew, I listened to their songs
as if they held some secret inner truth.
I didn't want to dream so all alone —

when Whitney Houston cried *How will I know?*
her voice so squeaky-resonant my own
falsetto (unabashedly, I sang

along) could hardly even touch its depths,
I wondered whether I would ever find
the love that in her music video

burst smiling out at her from closet doors
and every gaily-painted window frame.
I watched her, worried I would die alone,

my parents' quiet, well-appointed house
entombing me in all they had achieved.
Pretending I was "radical" instead,

I judged she was too chic for them, so tall
and sinuous, her lipstick shades too pink
for kissing brutish men; I thought I knew

what Janet Jackson's *Pleasure Principle*
implied, and as I watched her grind her hips
I let my hand drift down between my thighs

to learn that sex was good enough alone.
I'd watch their videos on MTV
instead of going out, listening hungrily

to each CD, those silver mirrors lost
in which I saw my own rapt face. Because
Madonna's lyrics turned me on the most,

I'd listen to her songs in bed. Her hit
Into the Groove was hot enough to keep
me up all night—I'd set it on repeat,

the muscles in her voice massaging me,
my cock surging against my underwear.
I saw that I could cry alone—but still

I wished that I could love them, giving up
to them what they so much possessed: the strength
of throbbing synthesizers, pulsing lights,

the power of the rhythm to command
the heart. Before too long, I'd dance and twirl,
turn diva in my bathroom mirror, just

for me. I'd put on skin-tight jeans, blow-dry
my mousse-shaped hair, their music blaring all
through me. By then, I knew my parents thought

I was a queer. But looking at myself,
the movement of my lips as perfectly
in sync as Paula Abdul's prancing men,

I didn't care. I knew the melody
would never really set me free, I was
so utterly bereft. Yet *not* alone—

I knew a woman's voice was saving me.

A Poet's Education

for Derek Walcott

In fact, the classroom overlooked a street
That ended in a parking lot. "How quaint,"
I thought, a bit annoyed by my small desk.
I wasn't nervous; really, I was mad.
The river they referred to in the ad
Was far enough away—across Bay State
(The asphalt driveway had a name), then down
A grassy knoll that bordered Storrow Drive,
Beyond which, yes, one *"glimpsed"* the briny Charles—
I had a better chance of seeing Cuba

When gazing through that dingy window pane.
Of course, I wanted it to be romantic.
I wanted it to be unlike the stiff
Cadavers I had picked apart in labs
At Harvard Med; I wanted it to be *alive*,
The pounding pulse of iambs telling me
The body's truths in terms I understood.
I thought of Bishop, Lowell, Sexton, Plath—
Their workshops where the heart was bared without
The scalpel's blade, by instruments more sharp.
I wasn't nervous; serious for sure,

And proud I'd gotten in on scholarship.
I'd practiced how I'd introduce myself:
Respectfully, but not obsequious,
Perhaps a droll remark that showed I'd read
His work. The street and parking lot below
Provided little inspiration; still,
I thought I could impress him with a line
Or two of his I'd memorized. OK,
It's true, I was afraid of what he'd think

Of me—a careless dilettante, a wanna-be,
A fake, a ruffled-pink-sleeved *mariachi*
Who danced a bit too awkwardly, my feet

As much ungainly as they were too broad.
I worried that my peers had planned applause,
Or worse, cold apples polished to a shine
So bright that even a St. Lucian might
Be tempted. Mangos and cigars, the buzz
Of black mosquitos, the ocean's wish
To eat the island in its roaring jaws
Of waves—the fruits of my experience,
I hoped despite my nagging reticence,
Might still appeal. Each pun, each lively rhyme
Internalized by all my prison time—
Three years had passed when not a single word

Escaped from me to find the freedom of
The page—seemed ready for *his* medicine,
Seemed eager to express a kind of love,
To reinvent my lost Caribbean.
Then suddenly, as if on cue, he entered:
So dignified yet rumpled, stifling a yawn.
The words he spoke I wish I still remembered—
I've lost them in the spotlight that my awe
Directed toward the star that took the stage.
He outlined what his expectations were,
And warned us if we didn't read, his rage
Would be exacted on our timid verse
Which, by the way, we would not read in class—
Too many *finished* poems awaited us.

So much for my ingratiating chatter.
Hart Crane it was, then Auden, Dickinson—

We memorized, and scanned because it mattered—
Then Dante, xeroxed for us in Italian,
He challenged us to sound it out until
The language and the rhymes had filled
Our mouths with music we could taste, if not
Completely figure out. I learned to see
A loveliness that never tried to be,
The beauty in what once had seemed mundane—
What Mr. Bleaney took so properly
In hand, those prepositions ending lines
While Gunn's sad captains turned away.
Then Meredith's raw sonnets came one day:
So utterly redemptive, mordantly gay,

And written more as drama than as verse.
Performance! Even in a failing marriage,
The strange bravado to acknowledge
That poetry is singing in a voice
Undampened by its small, constricted space—
He said that resoluteness was the key.
My sonnets, sheaves of them, came back to me
With qualified encouragement, his face
Betraying humor when he said he hoped
I'd write a hundred more someday. I sulked
At first, convinced he thought my writing sucked.
The last of winter's dirty snow in heaps
Along that semblance of a street, I left
That day pretending I would not return.
Yet something stopped me. Something I had learned.
His dusty classroom beckoned, high aloft.

The Gift of AIDS 111

The Gift of AIDS

I saw you coming toward me with a gift.
You wore the slippers made of Kaposi's,
The gown of night and soaking sweats. You moved
As if you had been photographed—you blurred
The trees you passed before. You held the box
Inside your chest somehow, the ribbons were
Your arteries, its corners were your spine
And ribs. I pleaded with you, pleaded that
You give me what you hid from me; you laughed
Like it was not as painful as it was for you,
And suddenly the ground was silver clouds
And we were so in love it was impossible
That you were dead. I saw you coming close,
I saw you and you had a gift for me,
The gift of AIDS and blood that was your heart,
Your beating heart, your beating, beating heart.

The Abdominal Exam

Before the glimmer of his sunken eyes,
What question could I answer with my lies?

Digesting everything, it's all so plain
In him, his abdomen so thin the pain

Is almost visible. I probe the lump
His boyfriend noticed first, my left hand limp

Beneath the pressure of the right. With AIDS,
You have to think lymphoma — swollen nodes,

A tender spleen, the liver's jutting edge —
It strikes me suddenly I will oblige

This hunger that announces death is near,
And as I touch him, cold and cavalier,

The language of beneath the diaphragm
Has told me where it's coming from

And where I'm going, too: soft skin to rocks,
The body reveling until it wrecks

Against the same internal, hidden shoal,
The treasures we can't hide, our swallowed gold.

Darkest Purple

for Michael Canfield, d. 1995

Among the mourners gathered there were three
Young women, dressed in gold, black—*aubergine?*
Faint, high-pitched whistle from the bright CD

Inside its player (glimpsed on a table in
The corner): song rang out to my surprise,
More soothing than my strongest medicine.

I sniffed the scentless ninety-nine cent rose
I'd bought conveniently across the street;
Like anyone whose grief is all he knows,

Ungrateful, dumbly mad, disconsolate,
I wept, and listened. Mike, I thought of you.
The woman dressed in gold stood up to greet

A late arrival; I noticed that the other two
Held hands as if in love, as if the black
And purple—ashes, Kaposi's—could make a new

Protective color. One whose name was lack
And joy, one whose meaning was not to break.

The Changing Face of AIDS

I. The Ghost of Epidemiology

Aisha got it from her husband Dex
who'd shoot up with his friends when she was gone.
For Gloria, the unprotected sex
she traded for some crack was how. The guilt
of being negative brought Timothy
to that same place where on his knees he first
sucked Larry's cock—the blowing reeds like stilts
the high clouds teetered on above the Fens—
as if the nameless men who fucked his mouth
might help him speak to Larry once again.
I watch them all, but travel unannounced:
The ghost of epidemiology,

composite picture of their human needs,
believe me when I tell you what I know.
I am a kind of angel. Swollen nodes?
I've touched them with my icy fingertips.
The pitch of doubt? I've heard it in the bleat
of respirators churning through the night
so mindlessly it seems it's all for naught.
(I'm not the gentle, optimistic type.)
I'm here to tell you that you're dying now,
my voice disclosing what is underneath,
my voice, revising what you thought you knew.
My voice will drown you, like an undertow.

II. The New York Times, March 11, 1997

NEW AIDS DRUGS PROMISE CURE, New York—"Before
these drugs, the prospects for AIDS sufferers
were truly bleak," says Dr. Jack Kevor-
kian, a world-renowned authority
on terminal disease. Across the country,
hope has been felt even in hospices,
as end-stage wasting patients, formerly
expected to be dead, linger on. Says
AIDS victim "Timothy," infected through
promiscuous fellatio last year,
"It's like I was alive again." The truth
about these magic cocktails still seems murky,

however. Blaming government inaction,
ACT UP ex-members loudly criticized
the new advances, warning that reductions
in fear could lead to mass complacency.
In San Francisco, protesters drank bleach,
burned condoms, chanting "AIDS drugs not drugs aid!"
while blocking access to a library.
Still others blamed ACT UP for what they said
amounted to "collaboration." One
anonymous gay man was further quoted: "Size
is everything! More sex is hot sex!" None
of Mr. Clinton's stooges could be reached . . .

III. Monogamy Responds

I've lived with him for thirteen years. I cringe
at this confession: young and queer, I lack
"accomplishment." Gay friends have called it strange,
or worse, a shame, assimilationist,
self-loathing. Catholic, Latino, not
too buffed, and very shy, my other traits
are hardly what they'd call desirable;
I thought it a mistake when we first kissed,
that somehow I was really fooling him,
that he imagined I was someone else.
Monogamous since then, his heart my home,
I wonder, bracing for the next attack.

IV. The Pundits and the Experts Speak

If AIDS remains an epidemic in
the gay community, in spite of all
we know, the withheld blaming will begin.
Safe sex is oral sex! Gay marriages
would solve the social problems that gave rise
to AIDS. *The epidemic won't affect
the straight majority.* Gay men infect
each other irresponsibly. *Say yes
to AIDS, because resisting makes you mad.*
We found the cure! *The virus multiplies
despite suppression of the viral load.*
Most people don't believe in miracles.

V. Elegy for the AIDS Virus

How difficult it is to say goodbye
to scourge. For years we were obsessed with you,
your complex glycoproteins and your sly,
haphazard reproduction, your restraint
in your resistance, how you bathed so slight
yet fierce in our most intimate secretions.
We will remember you for generations;
electron micrographs of you seem quaint
already, in the moment of our victory.
How difficult it is to claim one's right
to living honestly. The honesty
you taught was nothing quite as true

as death, but neither was it final. Yes,
we vanquished you, with latex, protease
inhibitors, a little common sense—
what's that, you say? That some remain at risk?
How dare you try to threaten us again!
Of course, you'd like to make outrageous claims
that some behaviors haven't changed, that some
have not had access to the drugs that mask
your presence in the body. Difficult
it is, how very sad, to see you strain
(no pun intended) at response—our quilts,
our bravest poetry, our deaths with grace

and dignity have put you in your place.
This elegy itself renounces you,
as from this consciousness you've been erased.
The love for you was very strong, the hot
pursuits so many of us reveled in—
but what once felt like love was really not.
I hardly know what I will find to hate
as much as I have loved and hated what
you brought to bear upon my verse, the weight
of your oppression and the joys of truth.
How difficult it is—to face the white
of nothingness, of clarity. We win!

VI. Monogamy Gets Married

We planned the ceremony yesterday.
Location is Hawaii, some resort
with orchids in profusion, far away
enough that most our relatives won't come.
(The invitations should be elegant,
to make them wonder what they're missing.) You
in your tuxedo; I can wear one, too.
Officiating is a lesbian
of no particular denomination.
After a few most solemn vows, we'll want
to kiss without a moment's hesitation,
deeply, our mouths pure love (and not a port

of viral entry). Organ music then,
that washes over us in cleansing waves,
fat tears in everybody's eyes. That's when
we wonder what we've done, the nervousness
dissolving into—what? Elation, calm,
security? I look at you, my one
life's love, before the flash in unison
of other people's Polaroids: I guess
that I'm not blind, that I can really see
how finally I'm almost cured of all
that could destroy me. Pathogens, my needs,
the sunset's wound—your love is why I'm saved.

VII. The Ghost of Epidemiology Exacts Revenge

Perhaps it's childish, sending poisoned fruit
to them. (I don't believe in fairy tales;
I much prefer nonfiction.) Not invite
the likes of me to such a celebration?
Infuriating, certainly—and dumb.
Aisha, Timothy, and Dex, be heard!
The million others who shall die, awaken!
Infect this apple with a fact so hard
That no one can digest it. Free the rage
that comes from being told that you have failed,
that you're to blame for your destruction. Wage
with me a war against their hubris, come

and plant your kiss upon their cherry lips.
The epidemic *is* sustainable;
in each of you, and those you love, it lives.
They try to silence you with talk of cures,
they keep you at the margins, starved and chained,
invisible, rejected, naked, dead.
Yet only I can tell what lies ahead,
my scientific powers an allure
so irresistible that none shall doubt
again who is the fairest in the land.
No love can pay their monumental debt
of pride. The virus makes them mine to kill.

VIII. The New York Times, April 1, 1997

HAWAII — Two physicians wed today
before a gathering of family
and friends. Pretending they could have their way,
they said the vows they had composed themselves,
exchanging rings that symbolized their love.
The understated ceremony was,
if not conventional, at least a cause
of quiet celebration. Notables
reported to be in attendance were
that actress what's-her-name, maybe Tom Cruise,
and some generous soul who left before
they'd seen her gift: a perfect apple tree.

IX. The Failure of Empathy on Center Street

On Center Street, one finds it all: the art
of Africa, a lesbian café,
the Cuban–Puerto Rican mini-mart—
and even (past the post office) lilacs drooped
by heavy blooms, their fragrance everywhere.
It's spring in Boston, in this neighborhood
that has a name part-tropical but skewed
Midwest: Jamaica Plain, which sounds as odd
as what I've gathered in these bags for lunch.
Tostones, sushi, flavor-of-the-day
(one scoop) from JP Licks, and a huge bunch
of blushing grapes. So plentiful, yet scarce,

what one can find on Center Street: it's all
the poor can do to feed themselves, from what
I might discard. A woman in a shawl
that looks Peruvian stares hungrily my way,
and calls in Spanish with a stoic voice;
she's stationed just beside the lilacs, holds
a clutch of single roses wrapped in gold-
fringed cellophane. The prostitute with AIDS
(her name is Gloria, I think; she asked
me for a sandwich once, some apple juice)
ducks quick behind a dumpster, smoking crack,
as plentiful as ever on the street—

one really can get anything right here
on Center Street: AIDS, frozen yogurt, pills,
a bunch of seedless grapes, a can of beer,

a rose in cellophane for fifty cents.
A homeboy blasting rap outside the bank
is waiting for his test results, perhaps;
the clinic (which is free) next door still lacks
the space for waiting rooms with ambience
more hip and private than the "safer sex
meets velveteen" of chairs in crowded halls
with tacked-up posters. Wondering what's next,
I chew my sushi sullenly and think

what did we see in Center Street? It's all
much older dykes who stay at home—and dark
Dominicans and Mexicans who sell
whatever they can get their hands on. AIDS
is their disease these days, not ours. The men
shoot drugs, or sleep with prostitutes, then give
it to their wives and kids. I want to move
away from here, until my anger fades—
a bus groans by and belches fumes, a vast
black comma, punctuation to my irk.
It dissipates as promptly as the past.
And when it's gone, I realize it then,

that Center Street is anything but one
community in isolation. All
of us belong here, any could be stunned
by positive results, win lotteries,
lose everything because the bank foreclosed.
Impatiently, I count the languages
I overhear, almost convinced the breeze

that whistles gently through the lilacs is
the single song that once was known, both sound
and scent, the message unequivocal
in its polite refusal to be drowned:
Your heart is human. Never let it close.

X. Refinishing the Hardwood Floors

The day he came to give his estimate,
the rap he played came echoing amidst
the tall Victorians that line our street—
a jarring rumble, even in the cave
that they create. He wore a rumpled shirt
emblazoned with his name. "I'm Rafael—
it's nice to meet you, Dex." My hand seemed small
on shaking his, whose palm was etched and carved
with lines—it felt like corrugated steel.
We knew that he was ill; to do our part,
we try to offer jobs through special deals
for those in the community with AIDS.

He paused as we ascended, out of breath.
I wondered whether he was up to it:
our loft is huge, and traps the heat beneath
the skylights we put in last year. Besides—
the flecks of sawdust on the skeletal
black arms that braced him on the banister
were mixed with track marks, tiny dots of scars
along his veins. A loud dog barked outside,
which cued us to resume our climb. What changed,
so that I saw him shuffle down the hall,
delivered at its end to the airy stage,
cathedral-ceilinged, window panes so great

that in their frame his slender silhouette
seemed insignificant? He jotted down
some notes, unnerving me the longer that
he stayed. The room was getting hot, transformed

from what was heavenly beside the man
I loved (I felt the rush of it anew,
the thrill of making household plans with you),
to an approaching hell with Dex. His firm
touch interrupted me just then: inscribed
in shaky handwriting were figures penned
with, evident in their completeness, pride.
He told me he could start next week. At dawn

on the appointed day, he came with two
assistants. k.d. lang or Europop—
I wondered which CD would better do
to drown their racket out. Too frequently,
perhaps, I checked on them, my concentration
shot even worse by a recurrent thought:
a stranger in the house you and I bought.
The sanding led to toxic fumes; for three
long days we aired our new room's shiny floor
impatient to set foot in our creation.
I paid in cash, then rushed Dex out the door;
I felt so clean I cried, and couldn't stop.

XI. Monogamy Strays

Just once, I thought, *just once.* I know you're not
supposed to see it like it's obvious,
but I was certain as this guy was hot
that he was negative. His skin was perfect,
his muscles flashed like fish beneath the waves
of strobe lights. Why did I go out that night?
In Washington on business, missed my flight
back home—hotel or terminal, the prospects
for sleep seemed equally unpleasant. So,
I called an old acquaintance. *Misbehave?*
No way, I thought when he proposed we go
out cruising to some clubs, the both of us

old (that is, thirtysomething) married girls.
Resistance disappeared on entering
the pulsing mass of sweaty men—my world
of rules disintegrated into what's
in retrospect seemed more than primal need,
the name I gave to wanting him inside
of me, anonymous and hard, just once.
Just once—I watched him dancing, magnified
in my imagination to the size
of many men, the sum of all my long
fidelity's invented fucks. My eyes,
though unaccustomed to this kind of greed,

maintained their fix on him, until the rest
of me enabled an approach. Not once
did I pretend I wouldn't: merriest
of temporary widows, drinks between

us gleaming like vague futures, I bemoaned
the loss of lovers dead from AIDS, but claimed
I had resolved to live my life again.
Perhaps he felt some pity, or some pain;
he took my hand and walked me out, to air
whose clarity enveloped him like ice.
T-shirt balled in his fist, he dried his hair,
then toweled off his chest. Above, the moon

seemed dim compared to all the streetlights. *Yes,*
I thought again, *just once — he'll never know.*
Past laundromats, past closed conveniences,
we never said a word, not even when
he stopped and bought an apple from a guy
who hawked them from a crate, mute himself but for
his sign: he was a homeless veteran,
his price was fifty cents. Around the cor-
ner, after sharing just a couple bites
of it, his graceful, underhanded throw
dispatched the apple to a dumpster. Sight
betraying me, that darkened alleyway

was where he kissed me, covering my mouth
but not to stifle an objection — all
around me it was happening, my death
approaching, searching, not a punishment
but as deliberate and pleasuring
as his hands on my cock, my mouth on his,
as though when he was coming I was meant
to understand our inner languages —

just once, imploring on my knees, *just once*
I prayed as if for swiftness in the kill,
as if for food to save the starving, sense
to save me from myself, or anything

but what I harbored then. "You're positive —
right?" Suddenly, I knew. Unconsciously
I drew away, receding from the love
that moments back was all I needed to
survive. The last words that he said to me
were those, which also were the first; he turned,
then drifted on the alleyway's dark blues
back to the world he knew. My stomach churned,
expressing satisfaction and remorse
at once. The world I faced was mystery —
a new betrayal, freedom that I cursed.
For once, I was what I would always be.

XII. Last Act

Not epidemiology, not love,
not even poetry describes the life
that tries despite this cursed disease to thrive.
I'm terminal, yet healthy now; I die,
just more expensively and publicly
than most, though I will end in isolation.
The blood that warms my hands is my damnation . . .
Or maybe not. Perhaps it's all a lie,
pure fantasy, one big mistake. The test
results, in fact, were indeterminate.
I'm well, albeit my mortality
more visible, but still unmet by fate,
my heart restored that wasn't ever safe.

A Death Perplexing

And when you died, it was perplexing. Songs
Reversed so that they were no longer songs;
The death of you was so perplexing, none
But I could see that you were really gone.
You lived so quietly that near the end
I hardly recognized you as my friend.
Instead, you were my lover, bodiless
And yet a hungry lover nonetheless.
You feasted on my heart, and I on yours;
Your eyes were just the first this death of yours
Consumed, as soon you tasted mine. A death
Perplexing as the death of you—your death,
Not mine, your death the death it took some time
To see completely. At a loss, untamed,
My grief bears no explaining—I am dead,
A death perplexing as the life I lead.

Small Comfort

What else is there to say, when what I see
Recedes before my eyes? Internally,

I try to understand where they have gone—
A man with ribs so prominent his bones

Become a cage that holds his soul, a child
So small she seems entirely her smile,

A woman with grey breasts so sunken in
They disappear to wrinkled folds of skin—

I try to guess where AIDS is taking them,
To brightness only visible to some,

To rooms without the walls I lean against
When I'm exhausted by my audience

With death. The doctor in the hospital,
The nurse approaching with the urinal,

Through corridors illuminated day
And night, we've wondered how the next will die—

I wonder what to say when entering,
"Emergency" shrieking the world's gone wrong—

To such completeness written on his face,
To eyes so animate they seem misplaced:

He hardly breathes, yet asks to hold my hand
As both of us are given to the grand.

Drawing Blood

Today, I try to concentrate on veins.
I notice them on everyone I meet:
The thready passageways that bifurcate
And reconnect, the complicated vines

That find their way unerringly to heart
And brain. The woman at the hardware store,
The burly bus driver, the man before
Me waiting at the traffic light alert

And pointed as the needle I would use
To make my stick; whoever is its source,
The redness always startles me. How scarce
It seems, no matter what the type transfused,

How terrible its power is to give
Us life. The blood that makes its surge through me,
I want to waste it, swallow greedily,
Its drip as sinister as bats in caves,

My lips, my mouth its temporary vase
In which I rearrange the flowering
Of breath that are my stories. When I sing,
I bleed, my lungs the awful hemorrhage

Of wishing that we were the same inside.
Today, I study veins; the blood contained
In them, so utterly impossible to drain,
I dream is just a form of genocide

That hasn't been discovered yet, I dream
That blood itself is poisonous, it wants to kill
Its hapless vessels, eager, ready to spill,
To paint the world the color of a scream.

The X Files IV

Opposites Attract

Imagine that you're home alone. You're bored,
and while you're surfing on the Internet
you realize you never understood
your father's grief. You realize you can't
begin to understand the human rights
abuses China has been guilty of
for decades; soon, you start to think that life
is pretty pointless, even in the age
of Microsoft and MCI. You can't
believe you put up with your father's rage.
You realize you hate the Internet
because it has this quality of — what? —
no memory, no true imagination?
You hate its artificial spacelessness,
and hate (in retrospect) how easily
you downloaded that porn. How sad
the models seemed, erect in cyberspace,
those utterly so disembodied men.
That's when you realize you loved him, that
unhappy bastard who was never home.
You realize you lack imagination,
like he did; just like him, you hardly spoke.
You realize it's time to order food
for dinner, can't decide if you want Thai
or Chinese, can't decide if you want life.
You realize, again, you're home alone.
You start to surf the Internet, for lack
of anything more fun to do. It's late,
and staring into that bright screen, you know
you never will, you'll never get back home.

My Reasoning

Illogical, yet not illogical,
The world proceeds in fits toward its destruction.
The world is ready for it. At luncheons,
In killing fields, the unbelievable

Is happening: poached eggs, crushed children's skulls.
It isn't hard, it isn't criminal.
The world proceeds with what is possible.
You say you love me; sunlight seems a skill

That anyone could learn, so sensible,
So clear. We walk across a fallow field,
Wondering what we know, what we can feel.
You say the world is what's invisible,

As if the wind that clasps my throat were real,
As if anyone deserves miracles.
The world goes on, both indestructible
And so terribly, terribly fragile

I'm almost too afraid to step again.
You say you love me, like that's logical,
And stoop to pick a buttercup, so small
I could have crushed it, tiny yellow sun;

I know that something's happening to me—
That in this world, some things aren't possible.
I look at you and see you're very ill.
You dart away. The world moves, quietly.

Three Recent Films

1. Philadelphia

A homophobic lawyer takes his case:
When someone spots a lesion on his face,

The character Tom Hanks plays is abruptly fired
By the firm that made him partner. What he desires

Is more than mere acceptance (he is gay);
He wants respect, he wants to make them pay

A million dollars for the care he needs.
He is a victim, after all, of AIDS

Whose lover is so beautiful he is
Untouchable—face free of lesions, lips

Divinely parted, eyes averted from
The tragedy. Back home, my lover comes

Before I do—his semen runs across
My chest as I imagine myself lost

Inside a movie made by *us*, inside
A world where none of us had lived and died

So urgently, yet so misunderstood.
Retelling history, as if I could,

My movie would be sexy, passionate—
I realize my timing is too late,

But seeing him so concentrated by
Our act of love—his thigh between my thighs,

The gentle gliding of his tongue along
My fingers, then my nipples, to my tongue—

Is why, much later, when I rise to write
About the movie neither of us liked

My thoughts keep drifting to last night. To learn
Again, dear brother, what I've always known.

II. The Hunger

When Susan Sarandon and Catherine Deneuve
Make love, it is among the sexiest
Of love scenes ever filmed: the blood is best,
Its trickle delicate across the nerves,

So vivid one can almost taste the salt.
Remember how we watched, attentively
Like Bowie at the cello; desperate, free
From their imprisonment is how we felt.

The dream I had that night was similar
To an aesthetic of the film—I feared
I might be hungry violently for years.
Then, once I captured you, I would not care

At all. Dispassionate desire, the loss
Of you so painless it was all I could
Endure; it frightened me that sex so good
Resulted in the taste of blood. Across

The bed from me you slept so peacefully.
As if you did not care to dream. I fought
The urge to kill you with a kiss: our fate,
This love undying, was happening to me.

III. Kiss of the Spider Woman

Imprisoned in a dream I had,
My cellmate, William Hurt, went mad
While telling me his stories. Sad

And glamorous, so glamorous
I hardly could believe in us—
We fell in love. You'll say, of course,

Two men in prison have no choice.
But I could hear it in his voice.
And he in mine. I held him close

And whispered in his ear a tale
Of my own . . . *Their torture always fails—*
The two of us, we must prevail

To change the world in which we'll be
Released. No longer shall we see
Excuses for brutality;

Whatever words we had for love
Will suddenly not be enough!
Outside of prison, we shall live

Together reinventing hearts,
The beating dense as iron bars,
Reading the welts the prison guards

Have written on our chests . . . Until
That night, instead of dream, I'd kill
Cockroaches on my windowsill

And stare into the night (perhaps
What I was searching for was help
To write these words). I press my lips

To William Hurt's; we are insane
With lust, and somewhere in the pain
I see an island, miles of sand

And someone skipping on the beach.
All seems to be well out of reach.
The sea, articulate as speech,

Is saying what I think I hear.
The rest of it remains unclear.
I drown, which is like drinking tears

But it's a dream so no one knows
And as the sky begins to close
I recognize my face in his.

Marry Me

for Jorge

Imagine it's Hawaii many years
from now, and strolling on the golden beach
together, you smile that smile of yours

and say to me, "Happy Anniversary"
like it's so natural or something, like
you really mean it, and though it's scary

I look in your brown eyes where I've seen your heart
a million times before, and say, "Would you
marry me again?" You pause, and this is the best part,

you get down on your knees and say, "Please spend
the rest of your life with me," and I don't cry
when I notice the vein in your neck, the sand

caught in the corners of your mouth (it's windy)—
instead I say like it was poetry, "I will,"
just two plain words, but it sounds so fancy

and then I wear the sunlight on my skin
like a white wedding dress, before we kiss again.

Recognition

That night, while he was beaten, I was stretched
in sleep beside the man I love. I'd dreamed
like anybody does; my heart half-leapt
when I awoke to singing in the shower.
The semi-darkness promised to grow true;

it seemed that life was good, your voice like grace.
As unaware as I was, you were happy.
We fixed our breakfast as we always do.
I toasted bread, too mindful of the hour,
our dog beneath me thinking she's a puppy,

pushing her nose against me, begging treats.
While tears washed blood in streaks from off his face
before the muted dawn, I watched you grind
our coffee, spilling some like dirt across
the green Formica countertop. It felt

like joy, to watch your squint-eyed measuring—
two cups, not more, of glinting water in
the clear glass pot. The simple ritual
that marries light and liquid, elements
that somehow join us—then, you smiled, as if

to prove us safe, or that the trees outside
could recognize us. Somewhere else, the boy
lost hope. A bit annoyed, I wiped the grounds
you always leave behind; by then, they'd found
what first was taken for an animal

that hunters lashed against a barbed-wire fence.
We drove together to the hospital

and held each other's hands, as usual,
bracing ourselves for others' misery,
or maybe nothing in particular,

or something else we'd yet to learn to see.
The boy was dying, rushed by ambulance
across a stretch of frozen countryside.
You kissed me sneakily on going up,
our elevator empty but for us;

your love, I felt, was rising into me.
But later, when we learned with disbelief
how Matthew Shepard died from injuries
he suffered as a consequence of this
same love, I wondered whether I deserved

to die that way, incomprehensibly
as why you couldn't hold me while you cried;
I wondered whether he had touched us as
he left an unfamiliar world, and whether
what he found was anything like grace.

The Mental Status Exam

What is the color of the mind? Beneath
The cranium it's pinkish grey, with flecks
Of white mixed in. What is the mind's motif?
Depends on what you mean: it's either sex
Or it's a box, release or pessimism.
Remember these three things: ball, sorrow, red.
Count backwards, from one-hundred down by sevens.
What is the color of the mind? It's said
That love can conquer all — interpret, please.
And who's the President? What year is it?
The mind is timeless, dizzy, unscrupulous;
The mind is sometimes only dimly lit.
Just two more silly questions: Can you sing
For us? Do you remember those three things?

The X Files

In search of them—the aliens we don't
know whether we should fear or hate—the stars
look puzzled by the gruesome murder scene.
I want to love them, touch them, but I can't.
The world I live in seems as damned as theirs.
The government denies all knowledge. Soon

the terrible conspiracy begins
unraveling; the aliens we hate
and fear are colonizing us the way
that cancer does. The stars, forever in
the kind of conflict desire can create,
look puzzled when they recognize its face.

We search, we search, for something that we think
is killing us. The cancer in a gland,
the alien with terrible black eyes,
the government whose politicians stink
of some conspiracy. Here is my hand,
Mulder—take me. Here, Scully, is the lie—

destroy it. All of us are aliens
no other understands. The world is full
of stars like me, each one no universe
can hide. Once I was abducted. My sins
were all erased, but they were clinical
in their precision when they stole my voice.

Still Monogamous after Fourteen Years

Tonight I fell in love with not. I was
Not interested. No, I said, but felt
My palms refuse the dryness that was cool
And comforting to me for many years.
Unable to recall the places on

My tongue that once had tasted bitterness,
(Not sweetness, nor the delicate red lips
Of how another said he loved me), I
Descended into nothingness. Forget
That it was poetry, not sex, forget

Denial was the mechanism of
My errant heart. Because I fell in love—
Not with a face, but with a certain phrase,
A way of saying something so untrue
It almost was believable—I knew

The winter would be very long, not warm,
That not to die was also not to live;
I knew that anything I said was now a lie.
Though not was beautiful, he was to me
Not kind. I'll never, ever be the same.

Begging for Change in Winter

This season always makes me think of peace,
Or dream of it at least, as I ignore
The signs of its receding from the world:
The headlines' promise of another war,

Or dream of it at least, as I ignore
An unkempt man who begs for change, who keeps
The headlines' promise of another war.
The rich against the poor, it's me against

This unkempt man who begs for change, who keeps
Reminding me of my humanity.
The rich against the poor, it's me against
The forces of injustice, all alone.

Reminding me of my humanity,
My coffee burns my tongue. It hurts to drink
The forces of injustice. All alone
In bed last night, I dreamed this happy dream:

My coffee burns my tongue, it hurts to drink
Because I'm nearly dead from thirst and then
In bed—O last of nights!—I dreamed. This dream
Was like my dream of peace, except peace wins

Because there's no one dead from thirst. And then
The world was pure again, receiving gifts
And giving them. I toss the man my change.
This season always makes me question peace.

Last Rites

Exhaustion enters me, as winter does
The emptiness of January days:
With clarity. These trees, starved down to bones,
Seem barely able to withstand the weight
Of what I am resigned to call the truth.

Last night I watched it happen. It was death,
As usual and present as the view
Of downtown Boston from my patient's room.
Before the bleed, he pointed out for me
A wisp of smoke that rose like mystery

Against the certain, dusk-blue sky. "I pray,"
He whispered to me as I probed his liver,
My hands, as in I pressed, brought close together.
Outside, a siren dwindled to a sigh.
"Do you believe in Christ?" I tried to pry

The image of the smoke (which wasn't more
Than some exhaust from an anonymous
Brick chimney) from my dimming faith that was
At once incomprehensible as stars
And as unknowable as they were far,

Appearing just above the skyscrapers.
I watched them from beside his bed, the world
And all its lights less glorious somehow;
I wondered, heartlessly, at who we were.
I didn't pray—I had forgotten how—

And then it came. The torrent of his blood,
Unstanchable, in roaring waves so full

I was less horrified than plain amazed.
His life flared out in red before my eyes;
The clots that lingered in his mouth were slick

As cherry candies on his startled tongue.
He looked at me, as pale as I was dumb,
And faded to his final peace. With God?
I searched the skyline for his wisp of smoke,
But night had rendered it invisible.

Lorca

V

I Am Mrs. Lorca

for Kim Vaeth and John Vincent

Dark love is all I've ever known; the dance
is nearly over, but I think the world
will not allow another end. The lights

burn bright, and I am married to romance,
his eyes betraying secrets that his words
conceal. He never speaks to me at night,

our bed as arid as the flat interior
of Spain. I love him just the same, the way
he combs his hair straight back, his hands

so womanly in shape. I'd be his whore,
but I am not as young as this new day,
this century we dance around;

I'd be his son, but I am not as sad
as dying is, as any son of his
inherits only death's queer finery;

right now, instead, I'm only going mad,
the dance and any meaning that it has
dissolving to the perfect thing he sees.

Sonnets of Dark Love

for Marilyn Hacker, Richard Howard, and Robert Pinsky
translated from the Spanish of Federico García Lorca

Gongoran Sonnet in which the Poet Sends a Dove to His Beloved

I send this dove from Turia to you.
With such endearing eyes and whitest feathers,
he spreads love's fire, and also offers
the Grecian laurel that the flames consume.

His honest virtue and his supple throat
twice soiled by slime and scalding foam—
his tremors, frost and misty pearls combined—
bespeak the absence of your mouth. But wait,

just run your hands across his purity
and you will know his snowy melody,
as snowflakes swirl about and cloud your beauty.

Such is my heart—by night and through the day
deprived of you it cries pure melancholy,
imprisoned in dark love that will not die.

The Night of Sleepless Love

The night above us, with a full moon—
I set myself to crying while you laughed.
Disdain was like a god in you, aloft;
my fleeting protests, doves linked in a chain.

The night beneath us. Through windowpanes of shame,
I saw you sulk along the deepest distances;
what hurt you was the handful of agonies
dispersing your weak heart of sand to its grains.

The dawn united us beyond our bed,
our mouths together at an endless stream
of isolated blood still being bled—

the sun barged through the shuttered balcony
and living's chorus opened up the shroud
that cloaked my dying heart that was not free.

Love Sleeps in the Poet's Heart

You'll never understand my love for you,
because you dream inside me, fast asleep.
I hide you, persecuted though you weep,
from the penetrating steel voice of truth.

Normalcy stirs both flesh and blinding star,
and pierces even my despairing heart.
Confusing reasoning has eaten out
the wings on which your spirit fiercely soared:

onlookers who gather on the garden lawn
await your body and my bitter grieving,
their jumping horses made of light, green manes.

But go on sleeping now, my life, my dear.
Hear my smashed blood rebuke their violins!
See how they still must spy on us, so near!

Sonnet about the Letter

My innermost of loves, my waking death,
in vain I still await your written word,
watching as this flower wilts. I swear,
I'd give you up before I lose my sense.

It's air that is immortal; stone is dumb,
incapable of knowing shadow or
avoiding it. My deeply buried heart
rejects the frozen honey shed by the moon—

and yet I suffered over you. I gashed
my veins, at once a tiger and a bird,
white lilies dueling jaws about your waist.

So saturate my lunacy with words
or leave me finally to live in peace,
my soul's long night eternally devoid of stars.

untitled

O secret voice of my dark love,
O bleating lamb without wool! O wound!
O needle of honey, a camellia drowned!
O current without sea, city without walls above!

O boundless night with certain boundaries,
celestial mountain swelled with all distress!
O dog in my heart, persecuted voice!
O silence without limit, ripest iris!

Flee from me, hot voice of icy tone.
You mustn't force me in the underbrush
where, without fruit, flesh and the heavens moan—

depart the solid ivory of my temples,
take pity on me, carry off my anguish!
I am love! I am natural!

The Poet Tells the Truth

I want to cry in shame, admitting it
to you so you could love me, and make for me
a dusk of nightingales with your own tears,
with this dagger you are, with your kiss.

I want to kill the only witness here
to the strange assassination of my flowers,
convert my groans and soaking sweats forever
to mountains of the hardiest wheat.

This tangle of wanting you to love me seems
so never ending, always ablaze
beneath the old moon, the decrepit sun's beams:

What you won't give me, and I can't plead
of you, it all will go to death, which leaves
for even the trembling flesh little shade.

Love's Sores

This light, this all-devouring fire.
This sullen countryside around me.
This hurt endured for a single dream.
This anguish in the sky, the world, each hour.

The blood-soaked cry that decorates
my pulseless lyre, my lustful torch.
This thrust of the sea, like a punch—
in my heart, this scorpion that waits—

These are the wreaths of love, the bed of wounds
where sleeplessly I conjure up your presence
among the ruins of the heart they drowned,

and though I seek the peak of prudence,
I come instead to your heart's long valley sown
with hemlock, and the passion of bitter science.

The Poet Asks His Beloved about Cuenca's "The Enchanted City"

Did you like the city that drop by drop
was carved by water in the heart of the pines?
Did you see dreams and faces and walls of pain
and the road that the air scoured and whipped?

Did you see the blue crack of broken moon
that The Joker moistened with crystal and trills?
Have your fingertips been kissed by the quills
that crown with love that remotest stone?

Did you remember me when you achieved
the serpent's silence, made the prisoner
of crickets, as he suffered in the shade?

Didn't you see in the transparent air
the dahlia made of shame and joyous cries
that I sent you from my burning heart?

Sonnet of the Rose Wreath

This wreath! Hurry, it's killing me!
Weave it quickly! Sing, groan, sing!
In my throat, shadow is thickening
as January's thousand lights decrease.

Between the fact that you love me and I love you,
between star-filled air and earthquake,
the thicket of anemones can invoke
with a dark rustle an entire year.

Enjoy my wounds like the cool countryside,
and trample down the reeds beside my riverbeds.
Drink like honey the blood shed from my thigh.

But hurry! Once together, roses round our bed,
time's passage will discover us, destroyed,
this love disfiguring my mouth, my soul mauled.

Sonnet of the Sweet Complaint

I'm scared as I lose the miracles
that are your chiseled eyes, and how you speak
at night, as if pressing against my cheek
the solitary rose your breath recalls.

I don't deserve to stand this shore, a tree
no more, a branchless trunk. Worst of all,
no flowers, no clay—I am without materials
to satisfy the worms of my misery.

If you are my cross, and my dank disdain,
if you are my sunken treasure chest,
then surely I'm a dog in your dominion.

Let me decorate the water with my best.
Don't take from me what I once gained.
Leaves from my enraptured autumn still are left.

The Poet Speaks by Telephone to His Beloved

Your voice created an oasis in
that tiny wooden booth, where formerly
vast sand dunes filled my heart; south of my feet
passed spring, while north of my brow grew ferns.

Inside that narrow space, light took a step
and sang as if unmindful of the dawn;
for the first time, my yearning could turn on
all along the ceiling halos bright with hope.

Sweet and distant voice, poured out for me.
Sweet and distant voice, savored by me.
Distant and sweet voice, muffled quietly.

Distant as an injured, dark doe.
Sweet, like a sob in the snow.
Distant and sweet, like marrow deep in the bone.

A Note on the Translations

Written in 1935, not long before his brutal murder at the hands of Spanish fascists, Federico García Lorca's *Sonetos del Amor Oscuro* (Sonnets of Dark Love) are among his very few poems to concern themselves with the pleasures and problems of so-called received form; they are also the only ones to address explicitly his struggles with his homosexuality. That Lorca is considered today to rank among Spain's greatest poets seems unsurprising; he was born at the dawn of a new century and became a handsome young man who visited the United States, was an intimate of Salvador Dalí, and studied Shakespeare alongside of Góngora. His short life was spent searching for ways to reinvent Spanish poetry, to free it from its past while drawing on its rich traditions, and in doing so he expanded the entire scope of the lyric imagination.

Curiously, this fascinating sequence of sonnets has received little attention from previous translators of Lorca's work. A particularly severe obsession with this form, which ironically has its origins in the Romance languages, was enough to draw me to them: how to render in English, whose masters supposedly had "perfected" this love song of lowly minstrels and troubadours, what moved so *intuitively* in Spanish? I have spent years trying to make my English sound like Spanish, that elusive inner language of my lost childhood in Latin America; in writing poetry, such linguistic alchemy sometimes seemed possible. Yet beyond the challenge of the languages, what enticed me even more was the theme of these poems. Not so much their "queerness" itself, which is obvious enough, but rather their use of the form as a way to engender delicious frictions which themselves convey meaning. Throughout these difficult poems, Lorca's desire refuses to be contained, always full of the possibilities and uncertainties of the times in which he lived and created them. As a gay man facing a new millennium, one which has been ushered in by the brutal murder of a young gay person in my own nation's heartland, one which sees still threatened the basic human rights to love and to live freely, and with its arts community still facing censorship, the urgency of this project was all the more clear.

Federico García Lorca was a true diva—an incomparable artist whose birth was full of promise, whose life was full of passion, and whose death was full of the pain of a silence that ultimately gives way to his gorgeous, eternal music.

R.C.

Jamaica Plain, Massachusetts

1998

Photograph by Miriam Berkley

Rafael Campo teaches and practices medicine at Beth Israel Deaconess Medical Center and Harvard Medical School. His other volumes of poetry are *What the Body Told* (also published by Duke University Press), which was awarded a 1996 Lambda Literary Award, and *The Other Man Was Me: A Voyage to the New World*, which won the National Poetry Series Award. He is also the author of a collection of essays, *The Poetry of Healing: A Doctor's Education in Empathy, Identity, and Desire*, which received a Lambda Literary Award in 1997.

ging-in-Publication Data

Campo, Rafael.

Diva / Rafael Campo.

p.   cm.

Includes translated selections from: Sonetos del amor oscuro / Federico García Lorca.

ISBN 0-8223-2383-4 (alk. paper).   —   ISBN 0-8223-2417-2 (pbk. : alk. paper)

1. Hispanic Americans—Poetry.   2. Hispanic American gays—Poetry.   3. Gay
men—United States—Poetry.   4. Gays—Identity—Poetry.   5. AIDS (Disease)—
Patients—Treatment—Poetry.   I. García Lorca, Federico, 1898–1936. Sonetos del
amor oscuro. English. Selections.   II. Title.

PS3553.A4883D58   1999

811'.54—dc21   99-18342